CHIC

SIMPLE ®

Components

"The trouble with living in sin is
the shortage of closet space."

MISSY DIZICK

CHIC
SIMPLE ®
Components

S T O R A G E

ALFRED A. KNOPF   NEW YORK   1994

THIS IS A BORZOI BOOK
PUBLISHED BY ALFRED A. KNOPF, INC.

Copyright © 1994 by Chic Simple,
a partnership of
A Stonework, Ltd., and Kim Johnson Gross, Inc.

KIM JOHNSON GROSS   JEFF STONE

WRITTEN BY JENNIFER LISLE
PHOTOGRAPHS BY JAMES WOJCIK
STYLED BY SUSAN CLAIRE MALONEY

ART DIRECTION BY WAYNE WOLF
ICON ILLUSTRATION BY ERIC HANSON

Library of Congress Cataloging-in-Publication Data
Lisle, Jennifer.
Chic simple. Storage/[written by Jennifer Lisle; Kim Johnson Gross and
Jeff Stone, editors]. — 1st ed.
p. cm. — (Chic simple components)
ISBN 0-679-43222-1
1. Storage in the home. I. Gross, Kim Johnson. II. Stone, Jeff. III. Title.
IV. Title: Storage. V. Series.
TX309.L56 1994
648\8—dc20
94-35298
CIP

Printed and bound in Canada

CONTENTS

"The more you know, the less you need."

AUSTRALIAN ABORIGINAL SAYING

Chic Simple is a primer for living well but sensibly. It's for those who believe that quality of life comes not in accumulating things, but in paring down to the essentials. Chic Simple enables readers to bring value and style into their lives with economy and simplicity.

S T O R A G E

Storage is about restriction, discernment, memories, and, ultimately, freedom. It's about what you need, and what you have accumulated—and too often, what is this and why do I keep it? Everyone has the flash of "If I'm so smart, how come I have so much stuff?" This isn't a minimalist cry but the frustration of why won't my closet close. Storage is about efficiency, but we are complex creatures, and, in the final analysis, storage is also about having the freedom to archive what makes up one's life, from baseball cards to ruby slippers.

"The only menace is inertia."

ST. JOHN PERSE

THE HISTORY OF STORAGE
IS QUIRKY. THE DISCOVERY OF THE SHELF

WAS NOT A HIGH DARWINIAN MOMENT IN THE EVOLUTION of the species, and the use of the hook or branch was something we stole from watching the other primates in the neighborhood. What was important was what we chose to store—grains, furs for warmth, and even our dead. Storage evolved with our material lusts—from the Egyptians, who buried the Pharaohs with food and wine in earthen jars to enrich their afterlife, to the Dutch, who developed the kas, an armoire that housed precious tapestries. Only with the New England Shakers did the spiritual and profane coexist as they based their clean-lined storage designs on the belief that every form must reflect its function and that earthly things should represent heavenly order. Today, Rubbermaid™ has continued that tradition.

"I don't want to own anything that won't fit into my coffin."

FRED ALLEN

15TH CENTURY *Pilgrims store their Bibles and bedsheets in the same wooden case boxes they travel with.* **17TH CENTURY** *Puritan ministers read, write, and meditate in closets.* **18TH CENTURY** *The French become obsessed with secrecy and the armoire. Marie Antoinette stores her lovers behind trapdoors at Versailles. Napoleon stores his hand in his jacket. Shakers in America in 1774 build chairs with drawers underneath the seat.* **19TH CENTURY** *David Roentgen, German furniture maker, invents trap-drawer furniture.* **20TH CENTURY** *In 1944, Earl Tupper slaps together plastic shards from the factory floor and invents Tupperware™, but has no luck selling it until 1950, when Brownie Wise looks him in the eye and says, "You should have a party."*

Time. *Organize* is the verb of storage, and good use of time makes it active rather than passive. Take time to compose a routine to keep things in place so you don't waste time with the daily question "When will I get to that?" It doesn't have to be a grand plan. Use small pieces of time. For everyday things, it can become a graceful dance you practice over and over. Set up a system of dealing with things once; a trash can by the mailbox or desk for junk mail, a policy of purging computer files weekly, or a directive that nothing gets set down on the counter. The most important part is commitment—honoring the system once it's choreographed.

THE THREE THINGS YOU CAN DO WITH PAPER ON YOUR DESK

You can...
1. *Throw it away.*
2. *Respond to it.*
3. *File it away.*

GIVE ME FIVE MINUTES

1. *Clear refrigerator of left-overs.* 2. *Clear one kitchen surface.*
3. *Tie up newspapers to be recycled.* 4. *Put away dry cleaning.* 5. *Mend a broken cup with Krazy Glue.* 6. *Get rid of old catalogues.* 7. *Unload dishwasher.* 8. *Transfer coffee beans and rice into storage containers.*
9. *Strip a bed.*
10. *Make a bed.*

Space. You can acquire or discard things, but the total volume of space in a home is fixed and constant. Part of storage is understanding and visualizing space. What if instead of that empty corner a screen was there—what could go behind that screen? Think of airspace like a city developer; it's a valuable and underutilized commodity. Is there space for an additional shelf in a cabinet or room for a cabinet over a door? If half the wall is used for bookcases, why not concentrate the storage on that wall and use all of it? If wall space is valuable go subterranean, utilize the space under draped tables or beds. It's okay, no one will tell your mom, and if she visits and starts to poke around, ask if she's lost weight. The trick of good space utilization is to maintain the illusion of spaciousness. Space is controllable, your mother isn't.

> "Small rooms or dwellings set the mind in the right path, large ones cause it to go astray."
>
> LEONARDO DA VINCI

Recycle. Like the broom in "The Sorcerer's Apprentice," possessions accumulate with a terrifying exponential growth. Hall closets begin as simple alcoves and metamorphose into black holes that swallow up entire year's worth of coats and create weird hybrid creatures of old phonebooks, wool mufflers, and parts of board games. We all live in the daily conflict of hoarding and simultaneously trying to streamline and get rid of the excess. Accumulations come from our weaker side—the one that believes we will be the same size we were three years ago, that we look good in orange, and that we will have the time to untangle old venetian blind cords. Parting with possessions means casting off illusions, so get a friend to help you go through your things. Assign them human qualities and ask yourself, "Do I want to share my life with you?" If you're not sure, try to stick to certain rules: If you haven't worn it or used it in a year, get rid of it. Then go through your belongings again. Then do it one more time, and afterward dance the happy dance. You should feel lighter—the way you feel after a good haircut.

"A garage sale is basically when strangers come to your house and examine your personal belongings with undisguised contempt."

DAVE BARRY

Organize. The sister in *The Accidental Tourist* who stored her groceries in alphabetical order had entered a new world of organization, a very scary one. Organization doesn't have to be a big production. It can simply be a few guidelines that distinguish between *storage,* "a place for things," and *to stow,* "to put something away in its proper place." There is no absolute truth. The order you create should be grounded in whatever works for you. Efficiency can follow the logic of boat design, where no space is wasted, and all equipment is in close proximity to its function. A hierarchy of use can impose order. In other words, match frequency of use with how easy it is to get to the object. The first step is storing seldom-used or seasonal items together. Even when they're "seldom used," it helps if you can locate these items easily. If you wish to trim the Christmas tree again or use the electric toothbrush warranty, a functional retrieval system is essential. It can be as simple as marking boxes with their contents and utilizing file cabinets for important papers.

"We shape clay into a pot, but it is the emptiness inside that holds whatever we want."

TAO TE CHING

Systems. It's so seductive. Storage catalogues come in the mail, and everything featured seems to fit. There are never more books than shelves, stereo equipment never holds piles of CDs. But beware: Just because it looks neat doesn't mean it's right for you. Scrutinize your things: Decide what you want displayed or hidden. Recognize the versatility of your stuff and the many ways it can be stored. A shirt can be folded on a shelf, placed in a drawer, or hung in a closet. All systems boil down to three basic components: the hook (the coat hanger is like a portable hook), the container, and the shelf. These are the basics. The secret is figuring out which to use, when.

SHAKER LOGIC

Shaker sewing chairs stored supplies in drawers underneath the seat. Use the same logic to develop a system. Group like things together and store things where you're likely to be able to reach them.

There's no place like home. Assign them homes as soon as possible and they will be more likely to stay there.

Simple Storage. The humbleness of a box's origin—whether shoe box, cigar box, or orange crate—belies the satisfaction it provides as a basic storage device. Boxes can define a moment in history—that time when you liked cheap cigars or fancy rings. As a child, the act of choosing boxes, labeling them, and keeping things together in one place may have been the first time you experienced privacy or responsibility. Our love of boxes attests to our need for intimacy and mystery, for an inner life or secret past.

FOR A RAINY (REALLY RAINY) DAY
Photograph the contents of a shoe box and tape it to the exterior, making it easy to identify what's inside.

"Happiness in every box."

*United Retail Candy
Stores Slogan*

A JAR IS A JAR IS A JAR

*Consider using objects in unexpected ways. The humble
~son jar can transform, and be transformed. A row of jars can
~e spices or Cheerios or pencils. An elegant glass bottle can hold
~ dishwashing liquid so it need not be hidden under the sink.
Old suitcases can be stacked to make a bedside table and,
even, store little-used items.*

P E R S O N A L

This is where you *keep* everything. It's beyond private, it's inviolate. It's where you keep your inner child. You can do what *you* want here with no arguments except physics when mass overwhelms volume. Like natural laws, the rules of storage remain fairly constant: the first is always to question what you think you need. The second is if you *need* it, where does it go?

"You can't have everything.
Where would you put it?"

STEVEN WRIGHT

[*where to put* **CLOTHES** *see page 80*]

Clothes. There must be a correlation between the average amount of clothes any of us owns and the amount of time they spend on the floor. You always own enough clothes to cover the floor of your closet at any given time. A closet should be a sanctuary, not an encounter session with your foibles of taste and waistline. Arrange things based on what makes sense for you. A closet is a tool; take the time to think about how to use it. Keep only what you wear every day. Store seasonal items. Always keep an empty box on the closet floor for donations to the Salvation Army. This is where you can throw the item that doesn't fit or hasn't been worn in this decade. Use closet common sense—keep elements together in designated categories; style, color, fabric, weight are all sorting devices. Clothes should be double-hung whenever possible.

"The average person wears 20% of his or her wardrobe 80% of the time."

FULTON & HATCH, *It's Here . . . Somewhere*

Men. Motorized tie racks with built-in lights are fascinating—they are the electric carving knives of closets. A simple peg system in all its Shaker plainness manages to store an amazing number of ties, and one placed above the other can handle seasonal changes. Wall pegs and hooks should also store belts. These devices free hanging space to accommodate jackets and trousers. Ipso facto, guard the rod space. Suits are often double-hung, but you may prefer to use hangers that allow pants to hang from the cuff—there are hangers for suits that allow this option. One advantage is the lack of a crease at the knees.

BLACK AND BLUE
40 percent more men than women are color-blind, so color-coding one's clothes can help. When stacking sweaters or shirts on a shelf, remember that dark colors like navy, green, and black may be hard to distinguish from each other and should be kept separate.

STILL RAINING
Take Polaroids of various shirt-and-tie combinations and place them in a pocket of the coordinating suit. This can ease early-morning scrambles for just the right outfit.

[*where to put* **MEN'S CLOTHES** *see page 82*]

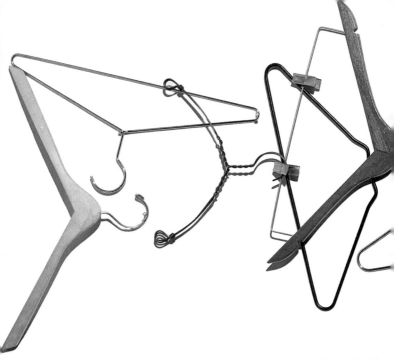

HANG-UPS. *It's virtually a science (subatomic theory?) to choose the right hanger to maintain clothes and facilitate their use. Generally, the heavier the garment, the heavier the hanger (rocket science). Wire hangers are less sturdy and more likely to snag clothes. Uniform plastic hangers are sturdy, as are contoured wooden suit hangers. Padded hangers work well for delicate fabrics like linen and silk, and cedar hangers can help repel moths. Scented hangers can be revived by spraying them with your own scents, but it's more practical to*

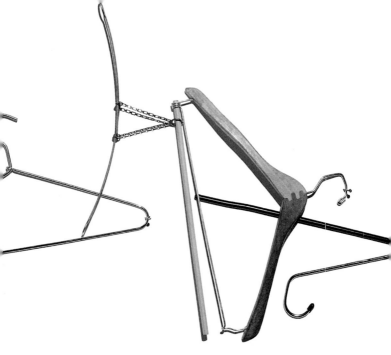

use hanging sachets. Two-piece outfits save horizontal space if they are hung together. Pants, unless they are knit, should always be hung. If you don't have the height for double-hanging, consider using swivel hangers that hold five or six pairs at once (you can always reuse these as TV antennas). The same is true for multiple-skirt hangers. Make sure blouses, skirts, and jackets are partly, if not completely, buttoned. Pants, however, should not be buttoned, but folded along creases instead.

Women. Imagine you've emerged from a long shower; you slip into a satin robe and make your way across the room to dress. You open your closet to discover that the tornado missed Dorothy's house and ended up here. This is not good. A closet is about storing and maintaining clothes. List your needs: what needs to be hung, what needs to be folded, and what needs to be easily and readily accessed. Try to hang by category and length to maximize space. Full-length items should hang at eye level. It helps to categorize them by use: work, casual, formal, love slave. Hang a full-length mirror inside the closet door or a wall nearby. Get your shoes off the floor and remember your waist may get smaller but your feet never do, so throw out all those glass slippers. Pay attention to fabrics—keep knits folded and flat. And get rid of plastic storage bags; they protect against dust and moths, but their chemicals can damage silk, linen, and white fabrics. Tissue or cloth bags are better if you need to protect something.

[*where to put* **WOMEN'S CLOTHES** *see page 82*]

Accessories. Accessories are all those things that don't fit on hangers. Remember the basics again: hook, container, or shelf. The crucial element is scale. Tame drawers (containers) by utilizing dividers. Folding underwear, socks, or stockings and stacking them upright between drawer dividers saves space and makes for easier access. Or if you're more casual, put baskets in the drawer. The back of the door is the most overlooked part of the closet. Here, shoe trees, belt hooks, and tie racks can be hung or built. Boxes can customize drawers and shelves by holding sweaters or cuff links—it's all in the scale.

CIGAR BOX
REDUX

For easy access, valuable jewelry is best between velvet- or felt-lined dividers, on adjustable trays, inside locked drawers. Hidden drawers and compartments can be built into columns or be masked by false drawer fronts. Locks will keep children and neighbors from your personal things, but even the most maladroit thief can break them. Read Edgar Allan Poe's "The Purloined Letter." For less frequent access, consider a safe, mounted in the wall or bolted to the floor. If space is an issue, consider renting a safe-deposit box at your local bank.

[*where to put* ACCESSORIES *see page 83*]

"All locks
are an
invitation to
thieves."

GASTON
BACHELARD

Kids. Experts say your child's closet should be a vehicle for teaching your child to organize space. In the real world, a kid thinks a closet is a place to hide stuff during the day and where the monsters hide at night. But you can make putting away and finding things easier and less frustrating for children. Have your child choose bright or decorative child-sized hangers. Access should be at your child's eye level. Decorative hooks hung low on the door or side of the closet are good for hanging robes, nightclothes, and towels. Keep shoes in bags hung on the door. Match toys and container size so big bins don't get tipped over in the hunt for small things.

LESS IS MORE
Remove some toys for a few months. Reintroduce them, and your child will delight in the discovery.

DANGER ZONE
1. *Toy bins should have slam-proof hinges.*
2. *Locking shelf supports keep adjustable shelves from tipping should your child turn them into a ladder.*
3. *Avoid sharp hooks . . . and dry-cleaner plastic bags.*

Bathroom. Step One. Remove everything not related to hygiene and grooming (this doesn't mean children or spouses). Step Two. Divide bathroom into activity zones, and analyze the kind of storage each requires. Plan storage places within appropriate zones, e.g., a makeup zone for makeup. When you come to see your bathroom this way, storage ideas evolve naturally. Assign specific items to drawers and install hooks along the walls or inside cabinets to facilitate the hanging of hair dryers and towels. Shelves in a medicine cabinet can be adjusted to hold more if same-sized items are stored together. Throw away old drugs.

BODILY FUNCTIONS

When organizing a bathroom, consider: 1. *Who uses the bathroom and when?* 2. *Is it shared by adults and children?* 3. *Do you put your makeup on in the bathroom? Standing? Sitting? While shaving?* 4. *Do you blow-dry your hair?* 5. *Are you claustrophobic?* 6. *Do you like to hand-wash lingerie, stockings, swimsuits, or exercise clothes in the bathroom sink?*

TICK TICK TICK

Regularly check medicine bottles for expiration dates. Cosmetics should also be checked. Even expensive makeup can go bad after six months.

[*where to put* **TOILETRIES** *see page 83*]

Linens. Throughout the ages, bedding and linens have been stored in wooden chests and trunks near the bed. This is still a good idea. Bedsheets can be stored in hollow ottomans, trunks at the foot of the bed, or compartments behind the headboard. The linen closet also serves the same function, but people often defeat its purpose by cramming it full of old towels and sheets. Weed through linens and discern what should be used as dropcloths, beach towels, or for washing the car. Then store them separately in the appropriate place. Your sheets should smell of sleep or sex, not pine-scented cleaning supplies. Try to store extra towels in the bathroom stacked on shelves or rolled up and placed in large baskets. A linen closet should have adequate ventilation and enough room for comforters to breathe. To keep it neat, avoid stacking too high; add more shelves instead. Pillows and duvets obviously have different spatial requirements than sheets. The initial effort to customize can save time and protect your investment.

[*where to put* **LINENS** *see page 84*]

Bedroom. It is rarely just for sleeping. A room of a thousand uses—from the romantic to the depressingly mundane—benefits from efficient storage. An aged Matisse kept paints and brushes always within reach and Proust had to have storage for his madeleines and milk. Whether it's a place for Dictaphones and laptops, audio/video remote controls, or massage oils and candles, space should be planned for each of them. Make use of every available inch, including the ceiling (hang the TV from there to free up surfaces). Create storage with recessed cubbyholes above the bed to save floor space, and buy nightstands that do more than collect dust.

RESERVOIR

It was a great place to hide your toys, and still is—utilize this pool of space under your bed. Purchase an assortment of bed boxes for out-of-season clothes or in-season erotica.

RESERVOIR TIP

To make condoms last longer, store them in a cool, dry place. Look for an expiration date; and be aware that the average shelf life for those with spermicide is only 2 years; condoms without spermicide last 3 years.

46

S H A R E D

It can be the living room, the kitchen, or the dining room—it's the place where things and people come crashing together, whether couples, roommates, families, or multiple personalities. It doesn't have to be a mess or a series of constant border skirmishes. It takes planning and dialogue. Work out your needs and discuss how they interact with your sharee.

"I hate women because they always know where things are."

JAMES THURBER

Kitchen. At one time, the kitchen was communal because the hearth held the promise of warmth, light, and food. Today, the kitchen has reemerged as a family center. What you store in your kitchen will depend on what you use your kitchen for—a gathering place for Wednesday-night poker, children's art projects, or amateur horticulture. If you actually cook in the kitchen, then take inventory. If the juicer is being used to hold phone messages, it's time to reexamine and recycle it. It's silly to have 42 food processor blades jumbled in a cupboard if you actually find it easier to use a chef's knife. Store only what you use, not what you think you'll use.

DON'T TOUCH
Keep knives sharp longer—prevent them from touching each other by storing in wood blocks or on magnetic strips.

5 EASY PIECES
When reorganizing kitchen space, consider assigning utensils numerical values, from 1 to 5, based on frequency of use, and give cabinets corresponding values.

HOW LONG
Whole coffee beans in sealed freezer bags last 3 to 4 months. Nuts, if kept cold, will last at least 6 months. Lager beer has a shelf life of 4 to 6 months if kept in the dark.

[*where to put in the* **KITCHEN** *see page 84*]

"To me a kitchen is just a big room to hold a toaster. That's the way I think of my apartment. Bedroom. Living room. Toaster room."

JERRY SEINFELD

Special Kitchen Storage. My mother always used her silverware for everyday use. She used to say that my father's next wife wasn't going to enjoy them. In other words, "good" tableware doesn't have to be stored in a museumlike installation. Base its location on frequency of use—whether it's daily, weekly, or yearly—and its degree of delicacy. Treat silver and china like arguing children—separate them. China designs over a glaze are more delicate than those underneath a glaze. Fabric and vinyl containers guard against moisture, chipping, and dust, yet fabric also allows ventilation and doesn't crack over time like vinyl.

CHINA CHIPS

1. *Rinse shortly after use, especially if acidic foods like vinegar or fruit are involved.* 2. *Avoid stacking without fabric liners.* 3. *Glazes chip if rubbed against equally hard surfaces.* 4. *Hang cups.* 5. *Use a mild dishwashing liquid for cleaning.* 6. *Abrasive powders can harm gold and silver decorations.* 7. *Dishwasher temperature should not exceed 140°F.* 8. *Hard-water spots can form on china if it is not towel-dried.*

Cleaning Supplies. Nothing seems to make women in commercials happier than a shiny clean home. True, a clean home can make one happy, but cleaning is a pain, and it gets worse if each time you have to look for everything. Make cleaning less of a chore: create a portable cleaning bucket or cart on wheels (or just move often). A complete set of supplies upstairs and down also may facilitate cleaning. Brooms, mops, dustpans are more efficiently stored if hung. Consider storing sponges and scrub brushes in a clay flowerpot or handsome dish.

KITCHEN GREENS
Trash drawers include separate recycling and composting areas.

BROCCOLI BLUES
Larger refrigerators now are built to house more fresh produce.

WHERE THE WILD THINGS ARE
Under the sink, hang utensils on the wall, build up areas in back to make bottles visible, install trays and shelves that slide out for easy access. Check expiration dates of cleaning products and lock cabinets if children are around.

"When spider webs unite, they can tie up a lion."
ETHIOPIAN PROVERB

[*where to put* **CLEANING SUPPLIES** *see page 84*]

Laundry. Laundry in Victorian times was done by women, in a separate house, which became a haven for romance and mystery. Now the person who opens a kitchen cupboard to reveal a small, energy-saving washer/dryer unit is a paragon of efficiency. While some may find a Zen moment in the pure act of sorting whites and darks into designated baskets, others want to get the job done quickly. So before reworking the space, consider your needs. **Divided** hampers shorten sorting time. Hampers on wheels roll easily to a faraway washer. A hinged table that mounts on the wall can be used for folding laundry. Since machines generally stand 12 inches from the wall, a shelf can be built in this space to allow for easy access to cleaning products. Wall-mounted ironing boards are worth their cost unless operating them requires a degree in mechanical engineering. Pull-out rods to hang clothes can be installed anywhere there's space. A Hide-A-Bed is probably suspicious.

> "Throughout history, the place where laundry gets done—be it by the creek or in a freestanding shed—has held out erotic possibilities."
>
> AKIKO BUSCH

Entertainment. We've rediscovered the home, the primal haven from the elements, but the stacks of video games in our home amusement arcade also make us realize the cocoon can be a very messy place. The lines between work, domestic necessity, and living in style are blurred. The PC works all day, playing games and doing homework, and the TV hooks us into the stereo system, the cable box, and the world. Now for entertainment storage we need to draw the line ourselves, creating storage zones around specific activity zones. Think convertibility and mold space with furniture. One chair is a study but two make a party.

[*where to put* **ENTERTAINMENT** *see page 85*]

CONDEMN OR CONDENSE
*Observe shelf-life rules for magazines,
catalogues, and newspapers. Keep
catalogues no longer than one season.
Throw out magazines monthly; clip
or tear articles you want to keep and
file them immediately. Game boxes
can be reinforced with masking tape
as soon as they are purchased, or
games can be condensed by taking
them out of boxes and storing pieces
in smaller boxes or clear plastic bags.*

LABEL

Label videos as soon
you tape them. Label c
gories by color and kee
master list by categor
Reusable floppy-disk la
that take erasable ink u
well for keeping track
frequently used files

BUYING IN

When shopping for
storing units, know the
size and type of product
you need beforehand.
Avoid wobbly CD towers
and awkward hexagonal
cubes. Make sure inexpen-
sive units sit solidly on
the floor and have at
least four shelves that are
deep enough, and
adjustable. Remember to
allow extra space for
future purchases.

Electronic Equipment. At some point, the compulsion to link up every possible component, as well as replace all your old LPs with CDs, can throw off entertainment-center harmony. To achieve balance in a freestanding unit: measure your TV, stereo, and VCR units. Place the middle of the TV screen at eye level. House the stereo above it, and Nintendo and other child-oriented components below. Bear in mind that exposure to dust, sunlight, and heat can be harmful to delicate electronics. Some components thrive in small cabinets, but others must be well ventilated. Separating components keeps them from interfering with each other and improves sound quality, so give them their space. Be liberal: buy large storing units and long cords, and make sure shelf materials are hardwood or strong particleboard. Surge protectors keep overloaded circuits from damaging entire systems. Measure and count tapes and CDs, and devise shelves and drawers to fit them around the big units. Use deep baskets or shelving next to the TV for frequently watched videotapes.

[*where to put* ELECTRONICS *see page 8 5*]

Desk. Desks used to be a tacit but clear indicator of office rank. The boss could always say, "Mine is bigger." At home, the only power dynamic is between the outlet board and fuse box, and desk size is a function of need. A desk at home may be communal or it may be designated for one person. It should be large enough to accommodate computer components. Many believe that the correlation between a clean work surface and worker productivity is high; some people also think that oysters are an aphrodisiac. It's all in the head, so do whatever makes sense to you. Mobile files underneath a desk provide easy access, as do storage cabinets above.

ORGANIZATION
MAN

In organizing an office or any space, it helps to know who you are. According to professional organizers, if you are right-brained (creative, immediate), the tendency may be to form emotional attachments to inanimate objects readily. Your instincts are to store things and to use space only in a horizontal way. Left-brained people, on the other hand, get less attached and aren't afraid of using vertical linear space.

Home Office. A home office is a source of power—the place where an individual thrives apart from the company family. The virtual office is possible anywhere there's a surface flat enough for a laptop computer and modem, whether it's a beach chair or kitchen counter. But not every home office is a transcendental space on the banks of Walden Pond. In fact, 80 percent of kitchens double as home offices. Whatever space restrictions you may have, outfit the area to accommodate your business needs. Whether you run a small kitchen design business or simply want a place to balance your check-

[*where to put in the* **HOME OFFICE** *see page 85*]

book, plan the space so it works best for you. Positioning your desk at the back of the room facing the door may give you a psychological advantage over those entering (time enough to turn off the solitaire game) or you may just need to stay away from the distractions of a window. The task stations you set up, whether mobile or stationary, will dictate storage location. Remember that a four-drawer file cabinet takes up no more floor space than a two-drawer model; broker the rest of the airspace in the room based on the same principle. Making ample space may be more virtual than physical. Some software, for example, houses dictionaries and compresses extra files.

ZONES

Community zoning restrictions dictate which floors are safe for waterbeds— and desks. Make sure file cabinets, desks, and chests are not too heavy for residential use.

MAGNETISM

With care, floppy disks should last decades. Sunlight, temperature extremes, and magnetic fields around any electrical device can demagnetize them. A metal box will protect them.

Sports. Consolidate the relics of trends past and the evidence of new resolutions. Take the lesson of the linen closet and create a sports closet. Keep handy and safe only what you really use and rotate each season. Consider categorizing by sport and bulk, hanging skis, bikes, and Rollerblades. Install some units low enough for easy access by children. Smaller bins accommodate accessories like kneepads and goggles. For fast packing, try keeping vacation duffel bags stocked with beach, ski, or camping equipment, plus appropriate clothes and accessories.

TUNING UP

Turn ski bindings to zero so they don't lose tension. Keep skis dry; to prevent oxidation, don't store them in the garage. Ski boots: Store in their original box. Stuff the boot with newspaper. Keep dry, with buckles at medium tension.

BICYCLES

Be sure to lubricate the chain after long-term storage. Tighten and lubricate brakes as well. Store your helmet, gloves, water bottles, and accesories with your bike.

ROLLERBLADES

Hang Rollerblades. Keep dry.

"Now it's the same room but everything's different."

NEIL FINN & TIM FINN

[*where to put* **SPORTS** *see page 86*]

HANG SAFELY

Most bike damage occurs because bikes tip over in the garage. Use a rack. Crossbar bike racks take up more room but are safer than those that suspend the bike by a wheel because the frame is designed to take the entire weight of the bike.

Garden Tools. Think of a garden shed as a state of mind—whether you work in the luxury of a greenhouse or on a shelf in the garage. A potting area need not be huge, only organized. Set up a table as close to plants as possible. Plants on a terrace can be tended to with tools that may be stashed in an outdoor bench with a removable cover. Or you may choose to use a basket that is easily portable. Try to hang small items on a wall in order to leave room on the floor for large pieces of equipment. For potting plants, a narrow table high enough so you don't have to bend works best. Stack terra-cotta pots and bags of fertilizer and potting soil on shelves above or below a table. If there are small children or curious animals around, stack harmful substances in airtight containers on shelves above the table or locked in a storage cabinet.

DON'T KEEP SEEDS WITH YARD SUPPLIES

Outdoor and garage temperature extremes reduce chances of seed germination and hasten deterioration. Keep seeds in labeled, airtight containers (e.g., glass canning jars) indoors.

[*where to put* **TOOLS** *see page 86*]

"I get so dirty."

GREG BROWN, *Bath Tub Blues*

Wet. Consider the mudroom, the room that makes the transition from outside world to indoor possible. Foul weather warrants an area with pegs or hooks to hang up wet coats and boots. Hooks for children's clothes should be hung low enough for children to reach. A rubber tray or slatted wooden tray can hold muddy boots while protecting the floor from puddles. The space underneath long coats can accommodate shelves or a low boot rack. Use space outside the closet to provide additional shelves, hooks, and a bench with drawers to help make the transition between outside and inside easier, whether you're returning from an arctic February expedition or a muddy walk in the park. This gateway to the outside world can also accommodate everyday gear: keys, shopping totes, and school bags.

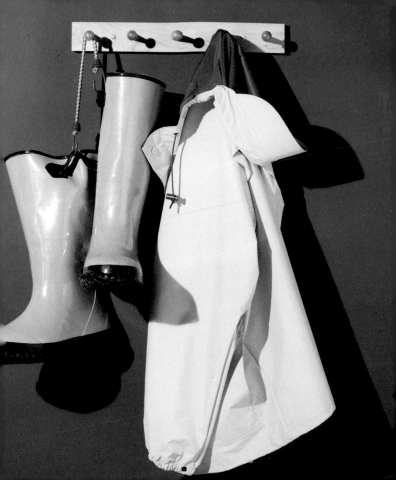

HOOKS. *It can be the first sentence that pulls you into a book, or the purest embodiment of instantaneous storage. Placed near the tub, it's the best place for a robe. When mounting a hook, consider the material it's made of: will it rust in a bathroom? Also consider the strength of the surface on which it's to be mounted. If the drywall is less than $1/2$ inch thick, mount the hooks themselves on a board that hangs on the wall so that the weight is more evenly distributed.*

"You've got to take the bull by the teeth."

SAMUEL GOLDWYN

Tools. The Shakers never broke out into full dance numbers, but if they had wanted to, they would have had plenty of floor space. They valued space, and hung tools, extra chairs, and shelves from pegs on the walls to make their rooms convertible. This concept makes for a funny looking living room but works great in the garage. Toolboxes are made for moving tools, not hiding them. Build a tool wall by hanging tools on a Peg-Board, then outline tools on the board so they will have a home. Don't be afraid to hang ladders, rakes, wheelbarrows, and garden hoses, but take into account how often you use them when deciding their location. Creating a drawer for nails, screws, and hooks can prevent you from buying unnecessary extras and make you see that the beauty of storage is not that you have everything, but that if you did, you would know where to find it.

"A flashlight is a great place to store dead batteries."

MILTON BERLE

[*where to put* **TOOLS** *see page 86*]

General Storage. An attic or basement can be a scary place. Not only is it a dark room where movie actresses always like to explore in sheer nighties as soon as the power fails, but it never feels quite organized. You can change all that. This is a place to store things that aren't necessarily obsolete but are just temporarily not in use. It may be necessary to make the space more user-friendly. Installing lights and repairing wall or ceiling damage are key first steps. If the area is temperate and dry, store off-season clothes, old china, books, antiques, and photographs there.

"Heredity is nothing bu

CHRISTO WARNING
Avoid wrapping in plastic. Its petroleum content bonds to silver over time, causing black marks—as do rubber bands. The gases given off by plastic will also yellow natural fabrics and fibers in rugs and apparel.

[*where to put* **SEASONAL ITEMS** *see page 87*]

Extreme changes in temperature and exposure to sun and dust can damage clothing, furniture, and equipment. Consider utilizing the space along walls to mount shelves or set up garment racks. Use old file cabinets to store income-tax returns, photographs, and diskettes, unless they are important enough to warrant the protection of a fireproof safe. Shelves can also be installed between open studs to maximize the use of smaller spaces. Boxes of like things and seasonal paraphernalia like holiday decorations should be grouped together and labeled.

ored environment."

NAME OF THE ROSE. *Keeping a record of what is stored where will bring remote storage space into focus. Number each box or bag clearly and boldly, and fill out a corresponding index card that lists contents. If clothing is inside, list sizes and styles.*

Where to put it. A fresh egg may have only one storage container, but for everything else, there are options. Use this as a guide to the myriad of storage possibilities already found, and as inspiration to boldly discover your own methods of storing where no man or woman has stored before.

CLOTHES

SHIRTS AND BLOUSES
1. Folded in tissue on a closet shelf.
2. Inside stacked plastic sweater drawers.
3. On shelves inside garment bags with clear plastic fronts. 4. On open canvas shelves that hang from a closet rod. 5. On wooden hangers; keep in plastic only for short term, or on padded satin hangers for silk and other delicate fabrics; otherwise, hangers should be plastic, wood, or steel coated with rubber. 6. On metal hooks or wooden pegs on the inside of a closet wall. 7. In the closet next to or with a matching suit or outfit.

T-SHIRTS
1. In deep drawers or wire-mesh drawers, rolled and placed upright.
2. Stacked horizontally on shelves.

3. Stacked in cubes. 4. Hung on hangers. 5. Hung from hooks. 6. Framed to commemorate an event.

WOOL SWEATERS
1. In cedar-lined, snag-free shelves or drawers, or in coated wire-mesh drawers, folded or rolled. 2. Folded over plastic hangers. 3. In wardrobe bags with shelves and see-through plastic windows. 4. In envelope-shaped clear vinyl and plastic bags. 5. In clear plastic boxes on shelves or under bed. 6. In stackable zippered garment bags.

PANTS
1. On plastic, metal, or wooden hangers, folded. 2. On a multiple hanger that swivels out. 3. On skirt-hanger clips. 4. Folded on a shelf. 5. Hung from hooks.

UNDERWEAR/LINGERIE

1. Folded, stacked in plastic dividers.
2. In lingerie bags. 3. In shoe caddies.
4. In mesh bags, each bag designated for garment type. 5. In scented drawers—spray scent lightly or leave scent samples in drawers. 6. In an open hatbox on a closet shelf. 7. In an open basket on a closet shelf. 8. Hung from notched hangers.
9. In plastic drawers.

SOCKS

1. In a drawer: Use plastic dividers. Fold socks and stand them upright with an edge showing. Categorize by use—work, sports, casual—or by color—from dark to light, or each color in a labeled divider for the color-blind. 2. In shoe caddies. 3. Inside shoes. 4. In wire-mesh drawers. 5. In baskets. 6. Inside plastic shoe boxes.

SUITS

1. Double-hung on wooden suit hangers.
2. In garment bags. 3. On collapsible garment racks in a makeshift closet.
4. On a telescoping rack.

SHOES

To preserve the life of a shoe, store with a cedar shoe tree inside.

1. In shoe caddies. 2. Stacked inside their boxes with a packet of salt to absorb moisture and a Polaroid photo of shoes taped to box (in the monsoon season). 3. On shoe racks placed on shelves or floor. 4. On the floor, underneath coordinating outfits.
5. In shoe bags. 6. In clear plastic boxes.
7. For the noncook, store shoes in kitchen cabinets or oven. 8. At the bottom of a garment bag with special-occasion dress, suit, or tuxedo, with shoe tree or tissue inside. 9. Inside individual stackable clear plastic shoe drawers. 10. On a shoe rack on rollers. 11. On an adjustable shoe carousel.
12. Store sandals in baskets. 13. Store thongs with beach equipment in a canvas duffel. 14. In wire-mesh drawers.
15. Hang athletic shoes from their laces on hooks inside the door. 16. Put slippers under your side of the bed. 17. In flannel, cotton, or any other breathable fabric shoe bags hung from hooks.
18. In portable shoe cubbies.

"If the shoe fits, you're not allowing for growth."

ROBERT N. COONS

BELTS

Do not store in pants, a skirt, or a dress as this could damage the fabric or shape of a garment.

1. On mounted racks. **2.** On hanger-shaped racks. **3.** On hooks. **4.** Inside shoe caddies.

HATS

1. Hung on individual hooks or pegs along a wall. **2.** Stacked on a shelf in the closet. **3.** Stacked or placed individually in hatboxes on a shelf or under a table. **4.** Hung from a coat tree.

GLOVES

If leather, make sure they are dry and clean before storing. Antique gloves should be wrapped in acid-free tissue or cotton muslin inside acid-free boxes.

1. Laid flat in drawer unit nearest the door. **2.** In clear plastic or labeled bins without lids on a shelf in the coat closet. **3.** Kids' mittens can be strung on a clothesline on the back of the closet door for easy drying.

MEN'S CLOTHES

TIES

Tie racks should be mounted in close proximity to suits. Consider the inside of a closet door or wall.

1. On revolving tie carousels. **2.** On over-the-door racks. **3.** On rod racks. **4.** On telescoping racks. **5.** Rolled and placed in plastic dividers.

WOMEN'S CLOTHES

DRESSES

If made of a knitted or wrinkle-free fabric, consider folding or rolling to place on a shelf or in a drawer.

1. On plastic, metal, or contoured wood hangers. **2.** On padded hangers, with tissue in sleeves. **3.** Hung inside out if fabric is natural.

SKIRTS

1. On a single hanger with clips.
2. On metal multiple-skirt hangers with rubber clips. **3.** Hung under suit jacket or matching blouse. **4.** For cotton skirts folded or rolled in a drawer or on a shelf. **5.** For long, wrinkle-free skirts, draped over a hanger.

STOCKINGS

Warning: Because they snag easily, stockings require special treatment. Make sure nonlaminated wood drawers are sanded well enough to be snag-free.

1. In a drawer, categorized by use or color. Your best bet is to roll them up into a tight ball, or knot them. Drawers can also be scented or cedar-lined. **2.** In mesh bags hung inside the closet door (also for dirty stockings—you can wash them inside the bag). **3.** In shoe caddies. **4.** In a plastic box. **5.** In a satin envelope. **6.** Inside shoes.

HANDBAGS

They should be snapped or zippered shut and stuffed with tissue to hold their shape.

1. Hung from their straps on hooks on a closet or bedroom wall. **2.** Standing upright on a closet shelf between vertical dividers. **3.** In clear plastic storage boxes on a shelf in the closet or under the bed. **4.** Standing upright in shallow wire-mesh drawers.

ACCESSORIES

JEWELRY

If valuable, store in a safe, vault, or locked drawer. Sterling pieces should be stored individually in velvet or felt pouches or compartments.

1. Rings, necklaces, and bracelets can be stored in a divider tray that separates pieces by category. **2.** Necklaces can be hung on decorative hooks or from a custom-designed closet rod. **3.** Small items can be stored in their original boxes in a shallow drawer.

TOILETRIES

BATH AND BODY PRODUCTS

1. Upright, in a shower caddie hung from the showerhead. **2.** On small corner shelves in the bathroom. **3.** On shelves installed above toilet. **4.** In a cabinet on a pull-out shelf below the sink. **5.** In clear plastic or labeled bins under the sink.

MAKEUP

1. In divided plastic trays on the vanity. **2.** In trays inside roll-out wire-mesh drawers in a cabinet under the sink. **3.** In a plastic tackle box with pull-out divided trays.

PENCILS, MASCARA, AND BRUSHES
1. Upright, in a decorative glass or small vase on the vanity. 2. In a portable pencil case in a drawer.

LINENS

TOWELS
1. Rolled, placed upright in baskets.
2. Rolled or folded, stacked horizontally.
3. Hung from a coat tree. 4. Inside an empty wine rack. 5. On hooks.
6. On towel rods.

BED LINENS
They should be cleaned thoroughly and kept in a dark, ventilated room. Folded and stacked, they can be placed:

1. On a shelf. 2. In a hollow ottoman near the bed. 3. Inside a hollow headboard.
4. In boxes with wheels under the bed.
5. Rolled in acid-free tissue or a cotton muslin bedsheet around an acid-free cardboard tube in a warm, dry place.
6. Wrapped in cloth and placed in acid-free boxes. 7. In a trunk.

EXTRA PILLOWS
1. In boxes on wheels under the bed.
2. Stacked on shelves in a clothes closet.
3. In extra drawers. 4. In a trunk or a locker. 5. In plastic or cloth bedding bags.

KITCHEN

CHINA
1. Stacked in fabric cases separated by felt pieces. 2. In thick corrugated boxes.

SILVER
Should be stored individually.

1. In felt-lined drawers or cases near the table with slots for each piece. 2. In velvet pouches with separate compartments.
3. In jewelry travel cases.

APPLIANCES
1. In slide-out drawers and shelves in cupboards. 2. In mobile wire-mesh carts with drawers. 3. On mobile butcher-block tables and shelves. 4. Inside covered appliance garages that pull down from cupboards. 5. Hung from a wall. 6. On a countertop. 7. Installed under cupboards.

CLEANING SUPPLIES

1. In wire-mesh pull-out drawers underneath the kitchen sink. 2. In a plastic bucket under the sink. 3. On shelves or in drawers of a mobile utility cart. 4. In plastic bins on the shelves of a hallway closet.

ENTERTAINMENT

MAGAZINES AND NEWSPAPERS
1. On shallow magazine shelves.
2. In small racks by a reading chair.
3. In upright modular cubes by category on bookshelves. 4. In baskets.
5. In a recycling container.

BOOKS
1. In bookcases. 2. Freestanding with back ventilation. 3. In a low bookcase at the foot of the bed. 4. In bedside stand.
5. Inside a convertible ottoman.
6. In lawyer's bookcases with a glass front.
7. Underneath coffee tables.
8. Built into wall units under the stairs.
9. Stacked along the edges of a buffet table, counter, or piano. 10. On extra closet shelves. 11. On mounted shelves with bookends along hallways and stairways. 12. As support for a tabletop.
13. Boxed, stored in the attic.
14. Stacked against walls.

ELECTRONIC EQUIPMENT

TELEVISION
1. In a cabinet, entertainment center.
2. Suspended from the ceiling. 3. On a hydraulic lift that rises from a table, trunk, or closet. 4. On a mobile cart.

TAPES/COMPACT DISCS
By music category or alphabetically.

1. In mounted modular units. 2. On modular shelves. 3. In drawers with dividers, by category. 4. In CD or cassette columns, if made of sturdy laminated particleboard units; avoid freestanding one-size "towers." 5. In built-in modular units around the stereo cabinet. 6. In portable CD albums with plastic pages.
7. On bookshelves.

VIDEOTAPES
Label all unmarked tapes before storing.

1. On bookshelves with bookends.
2. In modular cubes for each category.
3. On a shelf under a mobile TV cart.

HOME OFFICE

FILES
1. Upright in a file holder on the desk or mounted to a board above the desk. 2. Horizontally in a stacking tray or wicker basket on shelves off or on the desk. 3. In a file drawer under or close to the desk. 4. Upright in paper-covered cardboard.

FILE BOXES

1. In a mobile file cart or trolley that slides under the desk. 2. In a vertical file drawer. 3. In a horizontal file drawer. 4. In wicker/portable file baskets. 5. Inside a wooden trunk or an ottoman converted to a file drawer.

FLOPPY DISKS

1. In plastic or metal disk boxes filed by category or date. 2. In wicker file bins. 3. In shallow desk or file drawers converted with dividers. 4. In diskette holders mounted to a board above the desk. 5. In old lunchboxes.

CHECKS

Stacked and grouped by month and year.
1. In old check boxes, stacked and labeled in drawers or on shelves in the attic. 2. Grouped with rubber bands, in file folders, in an attic file cabinet. 3. If valuable, in boxes in a floor safe. 4. In marked shoe boxes, cardboard, metal, or plastic.

SPORTS

BIKES

Keep them off the floor so they're less likely to be tipped over; tires last longer, too.
1. On a vertical wall rack, hung by the front wheel. 2. On a horizontal rack, hung by the crossbar. 3. Hung upside down by the wheels on hooks from the ceiling.

RACKETS, BATS, STICKS, RODS, SKATES, AND BLADES

1. Hung on sport-specific coated-metal hanging racks. 2. Hung on hooks on a wall or Peg-Board. 3. Upright in a rubber trash can in the closet.

MITTS

Store with a ball inside, wrapped with a rubber band.
1. Inside mesh bags that hang on a wall. 2. In bins. 3. On particleboard or wire-mesh shelves in a closet near the door.

HOME EXERCISE GEAR

To make exercising more appealing, keep water bottles, personal stereos, athletic shoes, pulse meters, hand weights, books, or remote-control devices near major exercise equipment.
1. In wire-mesh drawer units inside the closet. 2. In a tall wicker basket. 3. In a locker. 4. In a small chest of drawers.

TOOLS

1. Hung on the wall, in outlined spots on a Peg-Board. 2. In a drawer with dividers. 3. In plastic bins on metal shelving in the basement. 4. In a leather tool apron hung on the wall.

NUTS AND BOLTS

1. In a drawer inside labeled plastic Baggies. 2. In large labeled glass jars on shelves near the tools.

PHOTOGRAPHS

Quality paper preserves photos longer.

1. In albums. 2. In acid-free plastic envelopes in a file cabinet or in drawers in a warm, dry, temperature-stable environment. 3. In acid-free cardboard boxes away from the light. 4. In a vault. 5. Framed. 6. In scrapbooks.

SEASONAL ITEMS

Off-season storage makes selecting from your closet each morning easier by affording more space and cutting down on visual distraction. Storage method is dictated by the kind, shape, and fabric of the clothing as well as the space. Exposure to air, dust, moths, and sun can damage fabric. Zippered fabric garment bags protect antique or delicate clothes best. Plastic is okay for the short term but may make whites turn yellow. Try to store off-season items in remote areas. Space can be created with collapsible garment racks or rods installed in alcoves.

Make sure to remove all dry-cleaner plastic. Wrap in acid-free tissue or cotton muslin if silk, satin, lace, beaded, or sequined.

OFF-SEASON CLOTHES

1. In fabric garment bags set up in an extra room. 2. In boxes on wheels under bed. 3. On shelves in garment bags. 4. In clear plastic boxes stacked on closet shelves. 5. In drawers of extra dresser or trunk in an extra room. 6. In an old suitcase or trunk.

SUITCASES/DUFFELS

1. Standing upright or stacked horizontally on metal shelving in the attic. 2. Garment bags can be hung in the off-season clothes closet. 3. If rigid, cases can be stacked three or four high and used as a nightstand. 4. Duffel bags can be stowed in a trunk or a locker. 5. Leather bags, if empty, can be stuffed with tissue and stored upright, away from moisture, to maintain shape.

> "Inanimate objects are classified scientifically into three major categories— those that don't work, those that break down, and those that get lost."
>
> RUSSELL BAKER

first aid.

Whether it's the kitchen "junk" drawer that opens twice a minute or

a faraway attic that's a land-of-no-return for *National Geographic*s,

bridesmaids' dresses, and bongo boards, there's more to know about

making it a place for things. First aid first.

WHAT YOU SHOULD HAVE AROUND

FIRST AID KIT
Store one of these portable kits in the kitchen cupboard and bathroom cabinet. Kept in a water-resistant sport sack, they are also always ready to travel: their contents allow you to immobilize an arm, care for cuts, and treat minor burns.

For severe bleeding and burns: 1 pressure bandage 6", 1 gauze roller bandage 2" x 5 yards, 1 gauze pad 3" x 3"

For medium cuts and scrapes: 2 gauze pads 4" x 4", 4 benzalkonium swabs, 2 gauze roller bandages 2" x 5 yards

*For small cuts and scrapes:
6 benzalkonium swabs, 4 gauze pads 2" x 2",
10 plastic strips, 2 fingertip bandages,
2 knuckle bandages, 2 elastic adhesive pads,
2" x 3", 1 telfa/melolite 3" x 4"*

For immobilizing an arm: 1 triangular bandage with 2 safety pins

*Additional supplies: 12 safety pins,
1 adhesive tape 4" x 4 yards, 1 pair latex gloves, tweezers, scissors*

(Available at the American Red Cross)

BUILDING

Check the walls before trying to put up any shelf, hook, or wall unit. Most closet-shelf organizers are designed to go up against a half-inch drywall. If you don't have this, you may have to get your own hardware.

MEASURING UP

When planning a wardrobe closet, consider the following:

GUIDELINES FOR MEN'S CLOTHING

	Length	Thickness
Suit	38″–42″	3″ or more
Dress shirt	38″–42″	½″ or less; ¼″ if on a wire hanger
Polo/sport shirt	38″–42″	½″ or less
Folded pants	28″–32″	½″–¾″
Long-hanging	48″–54″	¾″–1″
Ties	30″–33″	same width as tie
Belts	38″–44″	1″–1½″

GUIDELINES FOR WOMEN'S CLOTHING

	Length	Thickness
Skirts	22″–44″	1″–1½″
Suits	22″–42″	1″–1⅔″
Blouses	30″–42″	1″–2″
Dresses	48″–66″	1″–2″
Jackets	28″–42″	1″–1⅔″
Bathrobes	48″–68″	1″–3″
Jumpsuits	62″–68″	1″–1½″
Slacks	46″–50″	1″–1½″
Shorts	22″–30″	1″–1½″
Evening gowns	62″–68″	1″–6″

HISTORIC PRESERVATION

For long-term preservation of fabric, there are several important considerations. Any environment you create will be amplified over time, so be careful to make it as acid- and chemical-free as possible. Most tissue paper contains chemicals that will eventually break down and give off gas. Use blue acid-free tissue to wrap a garment, and line the box for maximum protection. Make sure to pat out any creased or pleated areas so they don't wrinkle. Make sure the box is acid-free and has no lettering or clear acetate plastic viewing window because these things will also emit gas. Use plastic only if the gown is already completely wrapped in tissue. Fabric needs to breathe or it will harden into the shape in which it is folded, so it is important that the box not be hermetically sealed. Store as far away from light and humidity as possible.

WEDDING DRESSES

Before the wedding, make sure the dress is not left uncovered on or near natural or artificial light. This is especially important for any dress made of silk, silk satin, peau de soie, velvet, or lace because they can fade or discolor in a matter of hours. Beaded designs will also fade. Dry-cleaner plastic gives off chemicals and may discolor the fabric as well. The best cover is a "breathable" fabric like cotton muslin. A medium blue bedsheet also works well because it prevents exposure to damaging ultraviolet rays.

SHEETS

In storing antique linens like tablecloths and bath towels, make sure to have them thoroughly cleaned beforehand. Stains attract insects and bacteria, and some substances, like sugar, oxidize over time and turn dark brown. If the fabric is in a long sheet, roll it between layers of acid-free tissue over an acid-free tube. It is also important to check the tissue every year; some tissue doesn't last more than two years. You can also use bedsheets instead of tissue, as long as they have been washed a few times to remove resins.

MOTH MEAT

Storing clothes without cleaning them is like curing food for moths. Mothballs work best in small, tight spaces, but the parachlorobenzene they give off can leach color and cause respiratory problems, so be careful how you use them. Fabrics that are suspected of having a moth problem can sometimes be frozen to get rid of the pests. Also be careful of Vapona strips. They can be harmful.

FABRIC SPA

The ideal environment for storing fabric is a stable 70° to 72°F, with 50 to 55 percent relative humidity. There should also be adequate ventilation. Extreme fluctuations in temperature are harmful.

VIRTUAL CLOSET

If you have trouble visualizing spatial relations in your closet, there is now a software program called One Minute Storage Solutions, by Lee Rowan. You enter the measurements and quantities of your clothes as well as the dimensions of your closet into special computers located in home centers and hardware or specialty stores, and receive a printout listing recommended closet components.

HOT CLOSET

If you live in a warm climate, beware of particleboard shelving. Particleboard, which is made of chopped-up bits of wood, expands in high humidity and may cause boxes stacked on top to become glued there. This will not happen with ventilated shelving.

FIRE

In buying a fireproof safe, make sure it is tested to the industry standard, which requires the temperature inside the chamber to remain below 350°F for one hour. (Paper chars at 421°F.)

PHOTOS

Printed photographs are best preserved in albums. It is important that they be printed on good paper if they are to last. If they record valuable memories, keep them in a fireproof safe. Important negatives should also be kept in a safe. In selecting a safe, be aware that film emulsions on negatives need to be protected at the same level as computer disks. Sentry Media Chest safes are Underwriter Laboratory–tested to remain below 125°F for half an hour.

CARING FOR FINE CHINA

Rinse dishes if they cannot be washed soon after use. This is particularly important if acid foods such as fruit or vinegar have been used. Use care when stacking plates, as the jolting of heavy stacks can cause scratching of the glaze. Glazes are hard and not easily scratched with a knife, but materials of equal strength will scratch each other—a diamond will scratch another diamond. Hang cups on hooks. Stacking should be avoided wherever possible. Take care in choosing detergents for washing either by hand or dishwasher. Abrasive powders can harm gold and silver decorations. Wash your china in a dishwasher but be careful to use no more detergent than the amount recommended by the manufacturer. The water temperature should not exceed 140°F. The following detergents have been tested in the Wedgwood laboratory and may be recommended for use: Dishwasher All, Cascade, Calgonite.

Generally, if a decoration is under the glaze, it is virtually indestructible: if it is on the glaze (and many of the brighter colors can only be applied in this manner), it is as durable as science can make it, but it can be damaged by really unkind treatment.

TO PREVENT CHIPPING AND DUST

Use cloth and vinyl china protection bags and put a piece of felt between each plate.

STORING SILVER

Avoid wrapping in plastic or rubber bands. Keep all silver away from dampness and direct sunlight. Even a light bulb that shines directly on silverware will cause it to tarnish faster than if it were in the dark. Use an airtight chest if possible, avoiding storing in drawers that are frequently opened. Also be careful of storing silver in wood-surfaced places: woods contain acids that will mar the finish. Also avoid oak boxes—silver tarnishes faster in them. To remove tarnish, polish the silver with a soft cotton or flannel cloth and a brand-name liquid or paste silver polish. Dip polishes can harm intricately detailed pieces.

Never keep stainless steel and silverware in the same basket; direct contact can permanently damage the silver.

EASY GLIDER

If you are buying or building an entertainment center or dresser, look for blome glides. They allow the television or stereo-component drawers to extend two thirds of the way out of the cabinet.

Also, offset hinges allow doors to open 176 percent without seeing the butt of the hinge.

OUT OF THE WOODS

Hardwoods like cherry, oak, bird's-eye maple, and walnut are darker, denser, and may be better than softwoods like pine for entertainment centers because they are less susceptible to warping.

HOME OFFICE

The more electronic equipment and components you have, the more airspace and protection from sun and heat you will need. Providing grounded electrical service with a dedicated surge-protection outlet strip helps protect both you and your equipment.

FISH

Goldfish should be kept in water at 70° to 76°F. Tropical fish need water that is around 78°F. It can be slightly hotter or colder, but it needs to be stable and as free as possible of organic waste and acid content.

Keep fish food in a cool, dry place.

CEDAR CHIPS

Moths have a discerning palate; they feast only on natural fabrics. Cedar doesn't kill moths—it only repels them—but it is a natural substance without formaldehyde or other chemicals used in mothballs. Cedar also smells much better than mothballs and is easier to use. Cedar strips nailed inside a closet are an alternative to the cedar chest or cedar-lined closet. Cedar blocks do not have to be replaced; they only require sanding to freshen their smell.

STORAGE ENEMIES

Road race, cheesy resort bar, and corporate promotional T-shirts
Empty wire dry-cleaner hangers
Coffee mugs with Garfield cartoons
Old medicine pill bottles, jars of creams and ointments
Orphan socks
Old handbags
Old shampoo
Free-gift cosmetics
Travel supplies

PLASTIC

Dry-cleaner plastic keeps dust away but beware of moisture if the climate is humid or storage is likely to be long-term.

BASEMENTS AND ATTICS

Before storing valuable items in basements and attics, check carefully for leaks, dampness, and sunlight. Bags should be labeled on the outside with sizes, styles, and colors. A master list can then describe where it all is. Fold clothes or pack in tissue as neatly as possible, as most natural fabrics can stiffen and lose their drape over time.

SHAKY REASONS TO HOLD ON

1. *I paid for it.*

2. *I got it as a gift.*

3. *It still works.*

4. *It only needs this one little part.*

5. *It reminds me of my ex.*

6. *It might be valuable someday.*

7. *It might come back into style.*

8. *It's not mine.*

9. *I'm saving it for my children.*

where. From coat hangers to professional mayhem tamers, there are resources available to control, to organize, and to make peace with our clutter or prized possessions.

FREEDOM OF CHOICE

Even as the world shrinks and chain stores expand globally, there are plenty of locales where choice is limited, if there is any choice at all. However, most companies today can aid you in finding a store or even mail direct to you. The U.S. numbers listed below will help give you freedom of choice.

STORAGE RETAILERS

California Closet Co.	818/705-2300
The Container Store	800/733-3532
Crate & Barrel	800/323-5461
Equipto	800/323-0801
Hold Everything	800/421-2264
Lechters	201/481-1100
Sam Flax	212/620-3000
Smith & Hawken	800/776-3336
Staples	800/333-3330

SALVATION ARMY (REGIONAL HEADQUARTERS)

East	914/620-7200
West	310/541-4721
South	404/728-1300
Central	708/294-2188

Drop off clothes, furniture, and other household goods for receipt or call for pick-up service. Clothes donated are given to needy families or sold to support the Salvation Army's drug/alcohol rehabilitation centers; surplus clothing is given to families in disaster areas.

CALIFORNIA

ACME DISPLAY FIXTURE CO.
1057 South Olive Street
Los Angeles, CA 90015
213/749-9191
for catalogues
(Hangers and closet fixtures)

MAYFLOWER BOX & SHIP
8172 Sunset Boulevard
Los Angeles, CA 90046
213/656-5591
(Boxes and storage accessories)

BERKELEY DESIGN SHOP
2970 Adeline Street
Berkeley, CA 94703
510/841-5340
(Furniture that solves storage problems)

CALIFORNIA CLOSET CO.
3385 Robertson Place
Los Angeles, CA 90034
818/705-2300 for nearest location
(Custom closet design and installation)

CLOSET FACTORY
12800 South Broadway
Los Angeles, CA 90061
310/516-7000, call for nearest location
(Custom closet design and installation)

GEFEN SYSTEMS
6261 Variel Avenue
Suite C
Woodland Hills, CA 91367
800/545-6900 or
818/884-6294 in CA
(Software package that arranges your CDs and lets you select titles from your computer screen)

HOLD EVERYTHING
865 Market Street
San Francisco, CA 94103
415/546-0986 or
800/421-2264 to order
(Storage items and accessories)
Catalogue / Mail Order

KITCHEN ART
142 South Robertson Boulevard
Los Angeles, CA 90048
310/271-9499
(Kitchen storage supplies)

ORGANIZED DESIGNS
P.O. Box 6901
Beverly Hills, CA 90212
310/277-0499
(Smart storage units)

FLORIDA

CLOSET MAID
720 West 17th Street
Ocala, FL 34478
800/221-0641
(Closet and storage systems)

ILLINOIS

CRATE & BARREL
646 North Michigan Avenue
Chicago, IL 60611
312/787-5900 or
800/323-5461 for nearest location
(Home storage products)
Catalogue / Mail Order

EQUIPTO
225 South Highland Avenue
Aurora, IL 60507
800/323-0801
(All-steel shelving, racks, drawers, and bins)

NEW JERSEY

LECHTERS
1 Cape May Street
Harrison, NJ 07029
201/481-1100
(Closet organizing accessories)

NEW YORK

ABC CARPET & HOME
888 Broadway
New York, NY 10003
212/473-3000
*(Antique, reproduction, and
contemporary furnishings)*

AD HOC SOFTWARES
410 West Broadway
New York, NY 10012
212/925-2652
(Home storage systems)

BED, BATH & BEYOND
620 Sixth Avenue
New York, NY 10011
212/255-3550 or
516/424-1070
for U.S. listings
(Kitchen/bath organizers)

C.I.T.E.
100 Wooster Street
New York, NY 10012
212/431-7272
*(New and antique furniture
and accessories)*

DEAN & DELUCA
560 Broadway
New York, NY 10012
212/431-1691
*(Gourmet grocery and kitchen
supplies)*

GRACIOUS HOME
1220 Third Avenue
New York, NY 10021
212/517-6300 or
800/338-7809 outside New
York City
*(Storage for every inch of the
house)*

THE GRASS ROOTS
GARDEN
131 Spring Street
New York, NY 10012
212/226-2662
(Gardening supplies)

HOME STRETCH
ROBERTA WOLF
147 West 79th Street
New York, NY 10024
212/874-7849 (call for
consultation)
(Space planning and design)

KATE'S PAPERIE
561 Broadway
New York, NY 10012
212/941-9816
*(Paper storage boxes, file
cabinets)*

MIYA SHOJI AND
INTERIORS
109 West 17th Street
New York, NY 10011
212/243-6774
(Japanese screens)

SAM FLAX
12 West 20th Street
New York, NY 10011
212/620-3000
(Home office products)

STAPLES
1075 Sixth Avenue
New York, NY 10018
800/333-3330 for nearest
store
(Office supplies, storage boxes)

TERRA VERDE
TRADING CO.
120 Wooster Street
New York, NY 10012
212/925-4533
(Ecological home furnishings)

TREILLAGE
418 East 75th Street
New York, NY 10021
212/535-2288
*(Planters and containers,
garden-shelf organizers)*

ZONA
97 Greene Street
New York, NY 10012
212/925-6750
(Home furnishings)

CATALOGUE / MAIL ORDER

EXPOSURES
1 Memory Lane
P.O. Box 3615
Oshkosh, WI 54903
800/572-5750
(Storage for photographs)

LEVENGER
420 Commerce Drive
Delray Beach, FL 33445
800/545-0242
(Tools for serious readers)

SMITH & HAWKEN
Two Arbor Lane, Box 6900
Florence, KY 41022
800/776-3336
(Gardening tools and supplies)

INTERNATIONAL LISTINGS

France

PARIS

CALLIGRANE
4 & 6, rue du Pont-Louis-
Philippe
75004
48/04-31-89 or
40/27-00-74
(Home and office organizers)

CLIGNANCOURT FLEA
MARKET
Porte de Clignancourt
75018
(Flea market)

GOYARD
233, rue Saint-Honoré
75001
42/60-57-04
(Library trunks, hatboxes)

LA TUILE À LUP
35, rue Daubenton
75005
47/07-28-90
(Baskets, pottery, countryware)

MEUBLES PEINTS
32, rue de Sévigné
75004
42/77-54-60
*(18th- and 19th-century
Alsatian armoires)*

THOMAS BOOG
36, passage Jouffroy
75009
47/70-98-10
*(Antique boxes and silk
Victorian-like boxes)*

Great Britain

BRISTOL

BRISTOL CRAFT
CENTRE
6 Leonard Lane
BS1 1EA
272/297890
*(Work by leatherworkers and
weavers)*

CROYDON

IKEA LTD
Valley Park, Purley Way
CR0 4UZ
81/781-9003
(Contemporary furniture)

EAST SUSSEX

THOMAS SMITH TRUG
SHOP
Hailsham Road
Herstmonceux
323/832137
(Handcrafted English baskets
known as "trugs")

LONDON

AFTER NOAH
121 Upper Street
N1
71/359-4281
(Wicker baskets)

CATH KIDSTON
8 Clarendon Cross
W11
71/221-4000
(1950s Americana, containers)

THE GENERAL
TRADING COMPANY
144 Sloane Street
SW1X
71/730-0411
(Furnishings)

HABITAT
The Heal's Building
196 Tottenham Court Road
W1
71/631-3880
(Home furnishings)

HAYLOFT WOODWORK
3 Bond Street
W4
81/747-3510
(Custom-designed furniture
and storage units)

HOME AGE
Unit 2-3, Thomas Neal's
Earlham Street
WC2
71/379-5064
(Contemporary furniture)

IKEA LTD
2 Drury Way
North Circular Road
NW10 0TH
81/451-5566
(Contemporary furniture)

MUJI
26 Great Marlborough
Street
W1V 1HB
71/494-1197
(Generic life-style products
from Japan)

OLD PINE
594 Kings Road
SW6
71/736-5999
(Armoires, shelves, cupboards)

Japan

TOKYO

ACTUS
2-19-1 Shinjuku, BYGS
Building
Shinjuku-ku 160
3/3350-6011
(Closets, chests, bookshelves,
wardrobes)

IMON
2-6-16 Dogenzaka
Shibuya-ku 150
3/3462-1141
(Ready-made closets, chests,
and wardrobes)

MARUI SHINJUKU
INTERIOR
5-16-4 Shinjuku
Shinjuku-ku 160
3/3354-0101
(Unit storage furniture)

MUJIRUSHI RYOHIN
2-12-28 Kita-Aoyama
Minato-ku 107
3/3478-5800
(Wooden boxes, wire shelving)

SHIBUYA LOFT
21-1 Udagawacho
Shibuya-ku 150
3/3462-0111
(Closet storage, wire units)

RESOURCES

"Two approaches: 'Live fast, die young, and leave a good-looking corpse.' 'Go to the dry cleaner's, clean out the attic, and take out the garbage.'"

MICK STEVENS

ACKNOWLEDGMENTS

MANUFACTURER & RETAIL RESEARCH	Susan Claire Maloney
QUOTE RESEARCH	Lige Rushing & Kate Doyle Hooper
COPY EDITOR	Borden Elniff

AND SPECIAL THANKS TO: David Bashaw, Claire Bradley, Tony Chirico, M. Scott Cookson, Henry Daas, Lauri Del Commune, Michael Drazen, Deborah Freeman, Jane Friedman, Janice Goldklang, Jo-Anne Harrison, Patrick Higgins, Katherine Hourigan, Andy Hughes, Carol Janeway, Barbara Jones-Diggs, Nicholas Latimer, William Loverd, Anne McCormick, Dwyer McIntosh, Sonny Mehta, Anne Messitte, Amy Needle, Lan Nguyen, Mitchell Rosenbaum, Alicia Rush, Suzanne Smith, Anne-Lise Spitzer, Robin Swados, Aileen Tse, Shelley Wanger.

COMMUNICATIONS

The world has gotten smaller and faster but we still can only be in one place at a time, which is why we are anxious to hear from you. We would like your input on stores and products that have impressed you. We are always happy to answer any questions you have about items in the book, and of course we are interested in feedback about Chic Simple.

Our address is:

84 WOOSTER STREET • NEW YORK, NY 10012

fax **(212)343-9678**

Our E-mail address: **info@chicsimple.com**

Compuserve number: **72704,2346**

Stay in touch because "The more you know, the less you need."

KIM JOHNSON GROSS & JEFF STONE

TYPE

The text of this book was set in two typefaces: New Baskerville and Futura. The ITC version of **NEW BASKERVILLE** is called Baskerville, which itself is a facsimile reproduction of types cast from molds made by John Baskerville (1706–1775) from his designs. Baskerville's original face was one of the forerunners of the type style known to printers as the "modern face"—a "modern" of the period A.D. 1800. **FUTURA** was produced in 1928 by Paul Renner (1878–1956), former director of the Munich School of Design, for the Bauer Type Foundry. Futura is simple in design and wonderfully restful in reading. It has been widely used in advertising because of its even, modern appearance in mass and its harmony with a great variety of other modern types.

SEPARATION AND FILM PREPARATION BY
COLOR SYSTEMS
New Britain, Connecticut

PRINTED AND BOUND BY
FRIESEN PRINTERS
Altona, Manitoba, Canada

HARDWARE
Apple Macintosh Quadra 700 and 800 personal computers; APS Technologies Syquest Drives; MicroNet DAT Drive; SuperMac 21" Color Monitor; Radius PrecisionColor Display/20; Radius 24X series Video Board; Hewlett-Packard LaserJet 4, Supra Fax Modem; provided and maintained by Abacus Solutions, New York, New York.

SOFTWARE
QuarkXPress 3.3, Adobe Photoshop 2.5.1, Microsoft Word 5.1, FileMaker Pro 2.0, Adobe Illustrator 5.0.1

MUSICWARE
Steve Roach (*Dreamtime Return*), Sarah McLachlan (*Fumbling Towards Ecstasy*), sequences and hymns by Hildegard of Bingen (*A Feather on the Breath of God*), Ray Lynch (*Nothing above My Shoulders but the Evening*), Dead Can Dance (*Into the Labyrinth*), The Clash (*London Calling*), k.d. lang (*Even Cowgirls Get the Blues*), The Modern Jazz Quartet (*MJA40/Disc Three*), Liz Phair (*Exile in Guyville*), Jane's Addiction (*Jane's Addiction*), Milt Jackson and John Coltrane (*Bags & Trane*), The Best of The Velvet Underground (*Words and Music of Lou Reed*)

103

"In order to seek one's own direction, one must simplify the mechanics of ordinary, everyday life."

PLATO